9 STEPS TO WISDOM – A HANDBOOK

Compiled by Robin Gibbs

Illustrated by
Pernille Damgaard

9 STEPS TO WISDOM – A HANDBOOK

Published by
9 Steps Publishing
San Clemente, California
United States of America

www.9stepstowisdom.wordpress.com

Copyright © 2013

Manufactured in the United States of America

No part of this publication may be reproduced, stored in a retrieval system or transmitted in any form or by any means, electronic, mechanical, photocopying, recording, scanning or otherwise, except as permitted under Sections 107 or 108 of the 1976 United States Copyright Act, without either the prior written permission of the Publisher or authorization through payment of the apppropriate per copy fee.

Dedicated to my father W.A. "Bill" Gibbs, Jr. (BG)

A man with a great sense of humor and
a lot of patience

At some point in my life, I realized that my father's influence had crept solidly into my consciousness. Surprise! ……..
He had been teaching me to be strong in reserve and to measure success, not just in what I would gain, but in what I would preserve.

We live in a world that has less and less respect for the consideration of others and less and less concern for the importance of self-control. Nevertheless, these are wise and powerful disciplines. The advice was given to me as insight for personal growth and societal contribution.

Regardless of your political persuasion, your faith, your athletic ability, your possible success on Match.com, your GPA, how long you have lived, your yearly income, your contributions to charity, your birth order position, whether you like chocolate or vanilla, your Facebook status, if you are urban or suburban, your gender, how much you exercise, if you are retired or working………. practicing these steps will add value to your everyday life.

………yes, I am still working on all of them.

These nine steps apply to all of life's complexities

CONTENTS

1. Don't Be Impatient 9

2. Humor is Key 13

3. Discernment Leads to Good Decisions 17

4. The Best Things Don't Come Easy 21

5. Pay Attention 25

6. Acknowledge Others 29

7. Listen 33

8. Words Matter 37

9. Take Off The Blinders 41

Simple Step

1

1

Don't Be Impatient

Simple Step 1

"The detour sign is there for a reason"
–BG

The Lesson: Exhibit Patience

Any day and any situation will throw up roadblocks. For a good manager, a good friend or a good colleague, roadblocks become opportunities to show decision making and problem solving skills. Taking the opportunity to think creatively will set you apart from others.

*Patience can persuade a prince and
soft speech can break bones.* (Prov. 25:15)

Once you know it, practice makes perfect………….

1. Count to ten before reacting.
2. Listen without interrupting.
3. Have important conversations while sitting.
4. Don't make decisions when emotional.
5. Have a special song and sing it in your head for a calming effect.
6. Drink water.
7. Say a small prayer before opening your mouth.
8. If you need to take a detour, learn something new along the way.
9. Remember, only God can see around corners.

Simple Step

2

2

Humor is Key

Simple Step 2

"Highly intelligent people read the comic strips first"
–BG

The Lesson: Encourage a sense of humor in all situations

Appropriate humor can diffuse tension, develop camaraderie and spark creativity. Being able to laugh at situations and at yourself is a healthy approach to life. Humor shows an ability to think quickly on your feet, to assimilate disparate facts and to remain approachable. Humor does not negate the importance of seriousness, but it can put things in perspective.

A joyful heart is good medicine, but depression drains one's strength (Prov. 17:22)

Once you know it, practice makes perfect............

1. When you do something stupid, laugh at yourself.
2. When someone else does something stupid, laugh it off, don't criticize.
3. Find jokes or cartoons that speak to specific situations.
4. Make it a point to laugh hard at least twice a day.
5. Choose a favorite humorist.
6. Develop friendships with people who appreciate humor.
7. Don't take yourself too seriously.

Simple Step

3

3

Discernment Leads To Good Decisions

Simple Step 3

"If it's a good deal today, it's a good deal tomorrow"
–BG

The Lesson: Guard against expediency

Ethics and accountability are important considerations in any decision. Making an expedient decision is the easy way out and usually means the problem is only masked and will become even more difficult to fix in the future. Every decision has its consequences.

> *The end of something is better than its beginning. It is better to be patient than arrogant.* (Ecc.7:8)

Once you know it, practice makes perfect............

1. Weigh your options carefully.
2. Understand the consequences of your actions.
3. Only commit what you can afford.
4. Look at your actions ethically; the end does not justify the means.
5. Be willing to ask for help or counsel from a trusted source.
6. Be patient.

Simple Step

9 Steps to Wisdom – A Handbook

The Best Things Don't Come Easy

Simple Step 4

"Going to McDonald's doesn't make you a hamburger"
–BG

The Lesson: Maintain integrity

Be the definition of integrity and steadfastness. Your word is key. Maintaining your ideals, your ethics and your philosophies wherever you find yourself is often difficult but always critical. Claiming a belief or an ideal doesn't mean anything… you must study it, live it and practice it… do not just visit it when it is convenient nor deny it when you are challenged… neither approach speaks to integrity. People trust you when they realize you do what you say you will do and you don't bend the way the wind blows.

People with integrity walk safely, but those who follow crooked paths will slip and fall (Prov. 10:9)

Once you know it, practice makes perfect………….

1. Don't make empty promises.
2. Take responsibility for your mistakes.
3. Be on time.
4. Listen to the other point of view.
5. Don't make snap judgments.
6. Don't spread rumors.
7. Defend the helpless.
8. Don't follow the crowd because it is easy.
9. Be genuine.

Simple Step

5

5

Pay Attention

Simple Step 5

"People always like to talk about themselves"
–BG

The Lesson: Show interest in others

You will be amazed at how often others' interests may be similar to your own or may spark a new idea in you. Even the most aloof, cold or harsh person is interested in him/herself and can be communicated with on a new level when you know something about them. You may find yourself the only one who can actually have a productive relationship with a difficult client, a contrary employee, an impossible boss or a thoughtless friend.

*Like golden apples in silver settings,
so is a word spoken at the right time.* (Prov. 25:11)

Once you know it, practice makes perfect.............

1. Find out what the other person likes.
2. Share articles or notifications of lectures or shows that speak to their interest.
3. Express concern when appropriate.
4. Give a small gift "out of the blue" that relates to their interest.
5. Introduce them to someone who has the same interests or who wants to learn more.
6. Ask questions that allow them to "enlighten" you.

Simple Step

6

9 Steps to Wisdom – A Handbook

6

Acknowledge Others

Simple Step 6

"Compliment someone at least once a day"
–BG

The Lesson: It's not always about you

Complimenting others makes them feel good and lessens the focus on your personal universe.

Don't be selfish; don't try to impress others. Be humble, thinking of others as better than yourselves. Don't look out only for your own interests, but take an interest in others, too.
(Phil. 2:3-)

Once you know it, practice makes perfect…………

1. Refuse the impulse to make it all about you….allow others to be the focus of the conversation, the story or the idea.
2. Acknowledge a recent act or contribution verbally or with a note.
3. Remember birthdays and anniversaries.
4. Single out people to congratulate when in group settings.
5. Hand write notes of congratulations.
6. When you read an article or an announcement about someone, cut it out and send it to them with a note.
7. Acknowledge invitations with a response.
8. Write timely thank you notes.
9. Establish a reward system for people who work with you.

Simple Step

7

Listen

Simple Step 7

"A raised voice loses the battle"
—BG

The Lesson: Lead by example

This is adjunct to "he who speaks first loses". Regardless of when you speak, your approach is the key to diffusing a tense or emotional dialogue. Our first reaction is to go head-to-head into the fray, but an initial deep breath is more effective.

Sin is unavoidable when there is much talk, but whoever seals his lips is wise. (Prov. 10:19)

Once you know it, practice makes perfect…………

1. Don't speak, listen.
2. Acknowledge the opposing viewpoint.
3. When it is time to respond, do so with a low, soft but firm voice.
4. Don't equivocate, stick with the facts.
5. Use consistent eye contact.
6. Ask for clarification.
7. Don't shut-down.

Simple Step

8

8

Words Matter

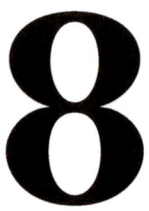

Simple Step 8

"Write it, sleep on it, edit it, send it"
–BG

The Lesson: Realize the power of perspective

Words have power… the power to alienate and the power to destroy or the power to persuade and the power to heal. Communication is a skill that requires discipline.

> *Whoever guards his mouth and his tongue keeps himself out of trouble.* (Prov. 21:23)

Once you know it, practice makes perfect…………

1. Never write down what you would be embarrassed to say.
2. Only put in writing what you would not mind sharing with many people, some of whom care about you.
3. Use proper grammar.
4. Don't use profanity.
5. Check your spelling.
6. Remember, what you write is discoverable in court…be honest.
7. If you have a complaint, always offer a solution.
8. Fewer, well-chosen words are better than a novelette.

Simple Step

9

9

Take Off The Blinders

Simple Step 9

"Lots of people in the cemetery had the right-of-way"
–BG
(My personal favorite)

The Lesson: Realize the "big picture"

Develop discernment and the ability to see the big picture. We often think because we can, we should. In life we can arrive at our goals more quickly and be more effective when we know how and when to sacrifice our "rights". Barreling through and demanding action or expecting blind allegiance can backfire in very destructive ways.

Listen to advice and accept discipline so that you may be wise the rest of your life. (Prov. 19:20)

Once you know it, practice makes perfect…………

1. Know your end-goal.
2. Listen to advice.
3. It may be legal, but not always ethical or moral.
4. Will it hurt others?
5. Just because you can, doesn't mean you should.
6. Consider the consequences.
7. Understand the greater good.
8. Be patient.

My father was a gentle man; successfull in business, strong in faith and quick with a very dry and pointed sense of humor. I never remember his raising his voice in anger and he never resorted to slang or obscenity to make a point. He was powerful in his reserve. His integrity was well-known. His convictions were clear and no one was ever surprised that his actions matched his words.

While simple, these steps can be difficult to master. Persistence is the key.

If you try, you will be amazed at the results.

Pernille Damgaard

Illustrator

Pernille Damgaard is a Danish illustrator living in Southern California, where she attended Laguna College of Art and Design studying illustration and Animation. Her interests range from book illustration to fine art and character design.

Her artwork incorporates everyday musings and observations on life, from the tiny details to the grand scheme.

View more work at www.pernilled.com

Notes